WHAT WE KNOW
SO FAR

micro fiction

Robert Scotellaro

BLUE LIGHT PRESS ◆ 1ST WORLD PUBLISHING

1ST WORLD
PUBLISHING

SAN FRANCISCO ◆ FAIRFIELD ◆ DELHI

WINNER OF THE 2015 BLUE LIGHT BOOK AWARD

WHAT WE KNOW SO FAR

Copyright ©2015 by Robert Scotellaro

1ST WORLD LIBRARY
PO Box 2211
Fairfield, Iowa 52556
www.1stworldpublishing.com

BLUE LIGHT PRESS
www.bluelightpress.com
Email: bluelightpress@aol.com

BOOK & COVER DESIGN
Melanie Gendron

COVER ART
Mike Worrall, *Seekers of the Truth*, oil on canvas, 2009

AUTHOR PHOTO
Diana Scott

FIRST EDITION

Library of Congress Control Number: 2015942371

ISBN 9781421837383

ACKNOWLEGEMENTS

Grateful acknowledgement is made to the following publications in which these works or earlier versions previously appeared:

"so much depends…" *The Journal of Compressed Creative Arts*
"In Lieu of Wings" *Boston Literary Magazine; The Medulla Review*
"Radio Sunglasses" *Mojave River Review*
"Big" *DOGZPLOT*
"Firewalker" *Flash: The International Short-Short Story Magazine*
"Skyline" *LITSNACK*
"A Change of Clothes" *100 Word Story*
"16 Wheeler" *Ragazine*
"God's Ex" *Apeiron Review*
"Kept" *DOGZPLOT*
"Sex & Death" *Boston Literary Magazine* (nominated for
    The Pushcart Prize)
"Transformer" *Vine Leaves Literary Journal; The Best of Vine Leaves
    Literary Journal*
"Pretty Much It" *Crack the Spine Literary Magazine*
"Interpreter of Dreams" *6S Anthology* (edited by Lydia Davis)
"Feasting On Crumbs" *Flash: The International Short-Short Story
    Magazine*
"Triple-Digits" *Flash: The International Short-Short Story Magazine*
"Cold Light" *Camroc Press Review*
"Evaporating Landscapes" *Boston Literary Magazine* (nominated for
    The Pushcart Prize)
"Preach" *Postcard Shorts*
"Superhero" *Flash: The International Short-Short Story Magazine*
"The Polygamist's Three Wives" *Mojave River Review*
"Her Life On Crooked" *Boston Literary Magazine*
"Some Like It Hot" *Flash: The International Short-Short Story
    Magazine*

"Have a Look" *Earl of Plaid Lit Journal*
"Many Skulls and Only One Piano" *Vine Leaves Literary Journal;*
    The Best of Vine Leaves Literary Journal
"Leo the Leviathan" *Postcard Shorts*
"Small Adjustments" *Blotterature Literary Magazine*
"Vitamin Express" *Blotterature Literary Magazine*
"Circle of Light" *Flash: The International Short-Short Story Magazine*
"Blood Watch" *Flash: The International Short-Short Story Magazine*
"Different/The Same" *Boston Literary Magazine*
"So They Said" *Microfiction Monday Magazine*
"Red Meat" *Camroc Press Review*
"Water in Still Life" *Vine Leaves Literary Journal; The Best of Vine
    Leaves Literary Journal*
"Zooland" *DOGZPLOT*
"Ancient Aliens" *Postcard Shorts*
"Ms. Fix-it" *Microfiction Monday Magazine*
"Prisoners of Momentum" *Postcard Shorts*
"Hand Shadows" *6S Anthology* (edited by Lydia Davis)
"The Specialist" *Postcard Shorts*
"So Much Changes, So Much Stays the Same" *Blotterature Literary
    Magazine*

for Diana—*Baby, you're the greatest!*

"You haven't seen a tree until you've seen its shadow from the sky."

—Amelia Earhart

CONTENTS

Pretty Much It

S he told him she saw a housepainter the other day in white coveralls with paint splatters on him of every possible color. How he was like a walking work of art. They were on the fire escape, drinking tequila straight from the bottle. And he was watching a flock of pigeons circle one of the tenements, where a man swinging a bamboo pole with a red rag at its end was churning the sky, seeming almost magically to be influencing their flight.

Art is where you find it, he told her. *Butchers wear white too. But red on white is pretty much it. Another kind of art, I suppose.*

Pork chops were on sale the other day, she said, after a long silence, taking the end of her dress and fanning her thighs with it. He tossed the empty bottle over the wrought iron bars and listened to it crash five stories below. There was Puerto Rican music coming from one of the open windows and a couple in their underwear, in a blue-walled room, dancing to it. *Pork chops are good*, he told her.

GOD'S EX

I'm living with God's ex. She's doing yoga, talking to me while standing on her head. Wants to clear out the guest room, teach pole dancing. *Isn't that for strippers?* I say.

Don't be narrow-minded, she tells me.

I'm reading a book about the San Francisco Earthquake of 1906. Use her panties for a bookmark. She's wearing my T-shirt, and it slides down to her chin. Five years ago she was nearly a nun. Weeks from her vows. It's kind of weird beating out God in anything. But here we are.

We could use the money, she says. She teaches workout classes downtown. She's fit. *You mean, like housewives trying to spice it up for hubby?* I tell her. She drops back down. *Don't be so cynical*, she says, *Christ. No fair bringing up the past*, I say. *It's popular*, she insists, *we should ride the trend. I don't know, Jan*, I tell her. *All that estrogen… the intrusion. Grow up*, she says, bends forehead to knees, sighs. And I realize I'm being a jerk. No way can I compete with the Big Guy by being an old stick-in-the-mud. And besides, extra cash never hurts. *Sure*, I tell her, *why not? Great*, she says. Gives me that big smile of hers she saves up—her benediction—then begins chanting *Ohmm…* My cue all communication has ended.

In 1906, I read, the earthquake devastated a mental hospital along with everything else. The frenzied patients were lassoed and tied to trees. There were fires everywhere, buildings collapsing. The gas, which had brightened so many homes, destroying a city. And I think, hey, I have beat out God, and there are women in leotards about to slide up and down a pole under my roof. How bad could it be?

RADIO SUNGLASSES

The mother ordered two. One for herself and one for her teenage daughter. *Radio Sunglasses.* The girl glared at the pair she'd just taken off. Music spitting out a staticky hiss. The mother kept hers on. Bobbing her head to her own static. Since the divorce, sleep had been a greased pig she chased. And the house was filling with items from late-night infomercials. *The Hurricane Spin Mop, Coffee Carousel, Hang a Bunch Hangers, The Lint Lizard...*

These are cool, the mother said.

Cool? The girl wondered if the pills were even working. And what was next? Next in the big picture, any picture at all. The girl was still in her cheerleader outfit, which had a small spot between the pleats *Stain-Buster!* couldn't tackle.

The mother tried to tap cigarette ash into a Coors bottlecap, but missed it completely. *Come ON,* she said. The girl rolled her eyes. Could hear the static banging against her mother's temples, her straw-dyed hair, her *Wonder One-Snap Rollers.*

SO MUCH DEPENDS...

We sat on a couch for wallflowers who sipped their drinks. She struck me as old-fashioned. Like she would have ridden a bicycle sidesaddle if she could. Outside, a blizzard banged at the windows. I told her I was a writer. She said, *Who isn't?* That she had a cousin who made up names for rodeo bulls. *Chicken on a Chain* was one. Said: *He writes.* The crowd thinned and took much of the body heat with them. She pulled out a joint. Asked what I wrote. When I said poetry, she said, *Who doesn't?*

We smoked it to the nub and went into the kitchen. Put our hands over the red coils of a toaster. Smiling when they touched. She said she had a favorite poem tattooed to her left cheek. Would I like to see it? I said, *Sure.* She lifted her dress, tugged at her panties. And there it was: Williams Carlos Williams' "The Red Wheelbarrow." In Courier. Like it was typed there. The image of the red wheelbarrow and the white chickens seemed so basic, so necessary to me.

Your turn, she said, putting herself back together, and our hands rose up again. I considered what it was I had to offer. Gazed out at a landscape losing its color. A snowman gaining way too much weight.

CIRCLE OF LIGHT

The man claimed he'd been a ringmaster for a traveling circus. Said he'd recite Joyce, with a mouthful of pebbles, to stay lingually fit. We were at a bar. There weren't any pebbles, so he used ice cubes, but was too drunk to remember the words. I imagined all the acts he must have introduced. The practiced talents that stunned and dazzled, once he exited that circle of light.

Instead, he decided to recite several garbled limericks, which had the barkeep in stitches. He loved kung fu movies; said they were the purest form of cinematic art. Good and evil played out with consummate balletic violence. Showed us a move or two with a drunkard's flair for ineptness, then sat back down and stared into his drink. Told us of the one that got away. Who wasn't a trapeze artist, and didn't do handstands on a pony in a tutu. But took care of the numbers in a back office, with thick legs, as he liked them, and cherry-red lips. He tried a mouthful of ice cubes again. Longfellow this time, but quickly spit them into a glass. Said he needed them to melt down a bit first. *Then you'll see*, he said.

MANY SKULLS AND ONLY ONE PIANO

Jane went with a biker who collected skulls. Miles from her cello growing up; her bed covered with stuffed animals, her pink, pink, pink. Felt it a ghoulish but compelling decor: the laughing skull on the TV, whose teeth chattered, the ashtrays, clocks, skull decal on the toilet seat, he always left up. The skull lamp she watched on his dresser—when she peeked out from under him—suspended there in the dark. His Harley had two. She liked the roar of it. The heads that turned when she was on back. All those skulls, concealed—decorated with skin and hair, lipstick and hats turned toward her.

She told him of a time when she played cello. A sorrowful beast she gave voice to. A sin she confessed. He grabbed a beer and took her into his garage. Past boards and pipes, to an old piano in the back. Two yellow keys dropped down like sinkholes. An ax on the floor, a big one, he picked up. She stiffened. Anticipating the wild swings; his massive body splintering it in a fury. Those skull-inked arms, shiny with sweat. But he tossed the ax aside, and sat—played Beatle songs, singing—looking up at her to sing along. *Hey Jude* and a few from *Sgt. Pepper*. And that's when she knew she would leave him.

DIFFERENT/THE SAME

My roommate was playing the accordion, leaning against the fridge. I'd broken up with Fran, was a bit pulpy and wanted to talk. When I told him how shitty I was feeling he squeezed off a polka, stamping his foot, saying what uplifting music it was. Told me to quit playing "Sad-Eyed Lady of the Lowlands" in my head. I wished he was an older sister.

He reached in the fridge and cracked open two cold ones. Drained half of his and belched. Went to the window, letting winter in, when I wanted it outside where it belonged. *Fuckin' A*, he said. *Fresh air.*

I had an uncle slap me hard once, when he caught me and a friend sword fighting with fluorescent light bulbs. *Jackass!* was all he said. *You could have blinded yourself, hon,* my aunt told me later, sliding over a plate of homemade cookies. They were both in boxes now. Different. The same.

My roommate put his can down and I lifted mine up. He played a festive tarantella; the perky bellows breathing in and out. Grinned over the top of it. I tapped my foot.

FEASTING ON CRUMBS

Gail picked up the sumo wrestler down at the wharf. His seeming tonnage, in a neat blue suit, draped over a chair in her kitchen. The doll furniture it became. He showed her a studio photo of himself in what looked like a diaper, crouched over in a menacing pose. She showed him a picture of her adult son. Diminutive in his thick fingers held gently, as though it were made of ash that might crumble, might blow away.

She told him of her dead husband. How he walked with a limp from the war. When she demonstrated, he laughed, not understanding, and she turned it into their little joke. He hardly spoke English, and they both used their hands and gestures as if playing charades to explain themselves. His hands and tortured English told of a child that died and a dancer from Osaka who betrayed him. Hers, of a lingering, but manageable hunger. Of the small meals now, that were all she required.

TRANSFORMER

A man's body had been slowly rising up in my older sister's: six-pack, breasts pushed off to the side and shrinking, turned into pecs. She sweated in front of the same mirror that held her fluffy dresses and princess wands. *Want one?* I asked, tapping out a cigarette as she grunted up another barbell. I sat in a cutesy chair by her vanity; a wasteland of make-up still cluttering it. *I'm in training*, she snapped. *Get a grip.*

Watching her become my brother was creeping me out; her biceps bigger than my thighs. The steroids, we all knew she was taking, blowing her up taut as a tire ready to explode. The Ouija board and our Monopoly and her lingering smiles replaced by sneers and strain and plump veins winding around her like a vine. The grease she'd rub on later, shining her up like a robot. The bikini she'd bulge out of; three tiny patches—two barely necessary. And when I asked again is if she wanted a smoke, her: *Get lost, squirt*, the only big sister thing, still familiar.

TRIPLE-DIGITS

He was a foreman in a toaster factory. Kept bringing them home. In every color. The kitchen counter had three. The rest were kept in the basement. *Wedding gifts*, he'd tell her. The day the divorce papers came through, she tossed them all: a clunky can-full. There'd been triple-digit heat for nearly a week, and looking at them gathered here and there had made her even hotter. She blasted heavy metal her father would have called *Sin Music*. Stood in her bra and panties in front of the refrigerator with the door open. With no one to complain about her letting the *cold air escape*.

SUPERHERO

I do not have a superpower. But an uncanny ability to finish other people's sentences. This, of course, does not translate to crime fighting; swinging from a spidery thread up or down a skyscraper. But flinging, instead, the populous at the *Peaceful Willow* rest home into a state of awe and wonder. Prying loose pieces of syntax from the rubble. The names of favorite shows and presidents, trapped in walls; particles of plaster trickling down as they strain to think.

Tapioca, I tell Mrs. Green, trying to describe what otherwise translates, descriptively, as "mud." Nobody's thinking I'm a bird, a plane; faster than a speeding bullet. Yet I see through walls.

Your Uncle, Jake, I say to another. *The tall one with the nice smile. That who?* And: *You mean, Rose Sunset? That pretty rouge you wear? Tyrone Power… Epson salts… Chrysanthemums…* I say. *You're certainly welcome. Close*, I say. *But, it's Roy. Oh, hon*, I say, *think nothing of it.*

THE POLYGAMIST'S THREE WIVES

The commune stood between a vast stretch of scrub oaks. A land purring with haiku, few noticed. The three women sat in the kitchen around a pie one of them had baked. Shared that each of them had been faking orgasms. The youngest one blushed. The middle wife was suddenly taken with the blades of the ceiling fan. The eldest, spit out a bit of pie as she laughed, which the baby on her lap stabbed with a finger and ate.

He sat in the next room. Looked over imperiously, and smiled. He was playing chess with his oldest, and not knowing which piece to move, he moved his coffee cup from one coffee ring to another. Off the kitchen, was the clomping sound of sneakers jogging around in the dryer, mixed with the wives' laughter. A bee flew in one window and out another, preferring the roses.

Her Life On Crooked

My sister (a liberal) is dating a cop named Ned. A hard-nosed bruiser who listens to conservative talk radio. Feels at times, like she is infiltrating a biker gang. Stalks about my kitchen with a bottle of Windex killing ants. *The scouts*, she says, *are the ones you want.* Those lone marauders with a megaphone. A trillion troops at the ready.

Why him? I ask. She shrugs. Gives a coquettish look, which means the sex is good. I follow in her wake with a paper towel, wiping up the saturated corpses. Think of the blind man I saw once, with his tie on crooked. Every mirror, a blackboard. What I feel she gazes into. Her life on crooked.

She shows me a picture of them on her iPhone. Small beside him. A barnacle on the side of a boulder. *Will you stop*, I say, the kitchen filling with fumes.

You get the scouts, she tells me, *it's clear sailing.* And I think, when is it ever clear sailing? You navigate the waves; their bumpy roads, make peace with wind. Remember when we were kids, looking up at shooting stars, how her half-eaten apple turned brown. Afraid she'd miss something. How small we were. How big the sky was.

In Lieu of Wings

Her legs are pretzeled together in a full lotus, and she's flapping her knees, hopping up and down. Leaving the carpet for an instant, landing butt-smashed several inches away. Trying to levitate. A workshop she's taken.

I look out the window I'm sitting by. A crow, from the crest of a clothesline pole, lands deftly atop a shingled roof. And gravity will not stand in its way. It does not long to ride a bike, or bang a tambourine. Monosyllabic, it will not change a single iamb from the songbirds fluffing out the tree next door. Beaming, she has propelled herself, gradually, halfway across the room.

If only we lived our lives in freeze frame, that snip of time off the ground could be more fully savored. Sweat dripping off the end of her nose, she continues to struggle up and down. *Down*, because gravity is a bitch. *Up*, because some things just seem to matter that much.

A CHANGE OF CLOTHES

Widows are beautiful, he thought. So covered in need they shimmered. This was his third. She lay under a sheet, which had a hole burnt into it earlier from a pot seed exploded from a joint. The size of a lizard's eye. *His suits suit you*, she said. *A little tight in the shoulders, but not so bad.* Her cat rubbed against him, as if nothing had changed. He turned this way and that in the long mirror. Reached for a silk suit on a hanger. She rolled another, using a credit card to separate the seeds out this time.

Some Like It Hot

It was my birthday and she was being *Marilyn*. Blonde wig and breathless, popping out of a gown stretched tight. And it was a kick watching her stay in character the whole day. Clicking around in those spiked heels I knew she hated. Bending over and watering the plants, turning to give me a wink. Not even taking any of it off for a quick one on the couch. Only once yelling at our cat, Roly-Poly, in her real voice for jumping on the table and licking icing off the cake. That steamy Marilyn voice returning quickly, as it leapt off. *You...bad...boy*, said sexy as I ever heard anything spoken. Telling me later, what I needed to pick up from the store: milk (said with a bubbly boil), butter (melting), ice cream (sizzling hot).

FIREWALKER

He'd taken a fire walking workshop in the desert. And now he lay in the ER with his feet bandaged, listening to the guy behind the curtain separating them. Those frenzied pleas to have the toilet seat removed (which was Crazy Glued, ambush-style, to his butt by his drug-addled son).

Thinking, what a colossal loser he was for not having the *faith* (or imaging he could) to walk over those red coals like the others. How mortifying it was when they had to drive him in, and his screams—Christ—the screams, his biggest declaration of failure. Just like his dad always confirmed when he didn't toe the line, or screwed up, because of it. Wished he could have Crazy Glued *him* to the seat—his throne—with his newspaper and magazine rack never out of reach.

The candy striper coming in now, all chipper, with a few copies of *People Magazine*, and glancing at those unworthy feet of his with an *Oh-you-poor-thing* look. That cute face, which had the amazing capacity for shouting: *Loser! Loser!* without ever moving its lips.

HAVE A LOOK

I date a fortune-teller with parrot-green eyes. She is lovely, but cryptic and seems to relish her words banging around in my head. We're in a hot air balloon above the Blue Mountains. *It will be like a pinched out wick to a stick of dynamite*, she says. *You mean, just in time?* I ask. *What, some illness? Do I need to see a doctor?*

She peers down through binoculars. The air is cold up here. I'd like to see what those green eyes see. *Never fire U-shaped arrows, no matter the target*, she tells me. *Is that what I'm doing. I mean, in life?* I say.

Ahh, she says, spotting something. *Beware, the pickpocket's hands. They are covered in grief. Christ!* I say, feeling for my wallet. But know it is my heart she means. Already hers. Damn it—those metaphors. Those inscrutable and wondrous mazes. She pulls the binoculars from her face and hands them to me. Says, *Have a look*. And there are those green eyes again.

LEO THE LEVIATHAN

His real name was Ben, but he was *Leo the Leviathan* in the ring. Wore a costume of fake seaweed, like endless green tassels and a plethora of stick-on barnacles. Even on his face. Begging her on his cell, in whispers, to reconsider. To take him back. His *Oh, baby, please baby*—coming out: *Uh-huh…uh-huh…* The phone so tiny in that scaly hand. And when she hung up on him, he wanted to weep. An ocean's worth. But Cyclops Cid, with his black eyepatch up over his head, was going through his locker across from him, looking for that talking turtle picture book his daughter wanted him to read. And besides, leviathans were not supposed to have tear ducts. Any *decent*, true-blooded leviathan that is.

SMALL ADJUSTMENTS

*Y*ou ever feel like you're a chew toy for the gods? I say. *You saying the gods are canine?* I smile. I shrug. We're on the boardwalk waiting to be photographed in one of those scene-props you stick your head through. Young heads filled with bric-a-brac, and diamonds, and farm equipment. Five months together; ice cream headaches intermittingly twisting our faces.

You think too much, she tells me, her head through one hole, mine the other. *You think?* I say. In a rocket ship; painted hands out of portholes, waving. Surrounded by stars in velvety space, heading for a distant planet. Our real hands at our sides like shovels. Deep in this earth.

BUG PORN

Curled over the microscope, he was watching cells divide in a harsh moon of light. *What are you up to?* she asked. She had come down the short flight of stairs, wearing a lacy red bra over her blouse. Just to be silly. To see where it might go.

Watching bug porn, he said, with one eye squinted shut. When he opened it and looked at her, he shook his head. Jotted something in a notebook. They were in the basement where he had his office, and she noticed a daddy longlegs above them on the low ceiling. Thought, how stunningly elegant it was; that tiny body ambling on slender threads. When she pointed it out, he stood quickly and swung his notebook, smashing it just inches from the light bulb.

Bug porn, she said after a pause, and could see he was pleased that she had registered his little joke. She reached back and unhooked her bra. Flung it over her shoulder, a dangling epaulet. Gazed up at the single leg stuck to the ceiling. Angled, just so, like a forward slash. With all of the surrounding grammar missing.

Nothing Like a Good Pair of Red Suspenders

The man outside the lamp shop snapped his red suspenders every time he said the word *Horrendous*. And he said it often. Was talking to a woman with an armload of groceries, never offering to help. Perhaps thinking it might interfere with the sheer drama with which he accented that word.

I was waiting at a bus stop and it was hot. I needed a job, and my gal had left me. It was horrendous. *This weather we're having*, he said, stretching out two elastic pyramids with his thumbs, repeated it all again.

And I wanted to jump him and steal his red suspenders. Go over to Julie's apartment and bang down the door. *You two-timin' fuck-wit!* I'd tell her right to her bug-eyed puss. *You no good roach-eating sleaze-ball!* I'd say. *You thoughtless, loosing-out-on-the-best-thing-you-ever-had-and-don't-even-know-it slime-bucket, shit-for-brains twit!* I'd rant. Snap! Snap! Snap!

WATER IN STILL LIFE

B ob did ice sculptures for fancy restaurants: seahorses, pea-
cocks, and swans. *Doesn't it make you a little sad?* she asked,
as he sat with his feet up on the coffee table, watching her
tropical fish bubbling around past pirate treasure in that giant tank
against the wall. Their neat little prison, he thought. *I mean, the
impermanence,* she went on. *All that work—that beautiful work—and
then what: a puddle?*

He watched the fish swirl and pause at the glass, as if fascinated
by the strange universe on the other side. He could hardly believe
nature had come up with so many amazing colors. When he fash-
ioned his peacocks, hueless against a tablecloth, color was only a
suggestion. The finely chiseled feathers, the details, merely conjur-
ing a *notion* of it. He turned his gaze, and clicked on the TV. *I don't
know,* he said. *Not really.* He switched through the channels without
hesitating. Too fast for her to make sense of what she was seeing.

Not really? she said. *Really?*

Right, he told her, feeling her eyes on him, as he pulled up the
TV guide from the side of the couch, and ran a quick finger down
the page.

PREACH

The preacher had one good eye and two prosthetic limbs. Dressed sharp enough to cut through an apple. That good eye swimming around in its socket like a shark sniffing out sin. You never got that he missed the parts he left behind, and nobody ever slept through one of his sermons. When he *laid hands on you*, even the fake one, it was said the devil hightailed it out of there, with no thought of a return trip.

Preach lived with his sister in a small house two blocks from the church. When she died, he took to drink. But that one eye of his, bloodshot and whiskey-glazed, never stopped banging around in there like it still meant business, and the devil had better not get any bright ideas to the contrary.

SEX & DEATH

I watch a cheetah on TV chasing down a gazelle, staying just enough behind to touch it with both paws now and then, waiting for its heart to explode. An easy kill plopped over into a blueplate special. The narrator could have just as easily been describing the Taj Mahal, or counting bricks on a brownstone in Harlem. Funny, what we come to accept. My daughter, when she was little, chomping on a mouthful of animal crackers—her cheeks ballooned out with the mashed up sum of her menagerie—nearly cried when she found a giraffe with its head missing. That long neck without a top. Took it so personally.

I switch the channel. A Mexican soap opera. I don't know a word of Spanish, but watch it anyway. No claws. At least not yet. Someone is cooking with plenty of garlic and its afterlife is working its way into the open window. There are two pigeons on the sill and it seems they are in love. The one, puffed up in a feathery profusion, is doing most of the talking. I turn from the enigma of Spanish to translate: *Let's screw. Let's screw. Let's screw.* Our lazy old cat, more refined, finds romance with a patch of sunlight. I turn back. A hand with painted nails, reaches up to a five o'clock shadow; two silver bracelets tinking down from her wrist. I decide to take up Spanish.

THE BUTTER CARVER

By any standard, Harold was a master butter carver. Sculpted an astronaut peering into a crater, a climber with an icicle beard atop Everest. Had a case full of awards and a letter from the mayor framed in his cold room. Was going over David and Goliath in his head, considering the scale, when she told him she was leaving. Had already packed her bags. *Butter*, she said, was for toast and hot buns. Slapped her butt in a tight pair of jeans with the flat of her hand. *You remember what buns are, right? Somewhere in that buttery brain of yours?*

He gazed at her for a moment, and then the door slammed. Followed by two thoughts: good riddance was the first. And how the hell was he going to fashion the sling, so tenuous, so elegantly slender with that small rock in it, was the second.

KEPT

I found the blow up doll crumpled under a bunch of shoes in his closet. He'd been in the home for several months and I'd managed to put off going through his stuff. The hats with a hint of that hair grease he fingered into the little that was left, the .22 rifle he showed us how to point at small animals, the binoculars he and his brother used to spy on nude hippies...

It was old and rubbery, collapsed in the corner. A stem I put to my lips to see who he'd kept company with all those years alone. She was a blonde. I tried to remember if his third or his fourth wife was a blonde.

It had a leak, maybe several. But it plumped up well enough for me to get a sense. Big breasts as he liked them. Cleopatra bangs. Wide eyes framed with black liner. And that mouth that never talked back, complained about his drinking. Bright red lips—nearly the color of that birdhouse he painted one summer—so many yards, so many birds ago.

SKYLINE

She'd always figured her husband for a spectacular death—a drop from 80 stories, still clutching a sandwich or a bucket of bolts—his face contorted, arms flailing. The closed casket later. Mentally, she planned for it. A single misstep, even though the other high steel workers called him *Glue Feet*, or a sudden gust of wind coming at him like a boulder down a mountain. Holding her breath each time the phone rang. Imagined the wake, the tall tales. Those steel-spined men remembering: that dropped wrench which nearly split a man in half—those crazy naps on girders, slender as thread—never spilling from a dream. The other wives consoling her—seeing them through a black veil, swallowing their dread, shaky but proud.

But never this: standing by the kitchen window watching a ruby-throated hummingbird by the feeder he put up days earlier. The garbage disposal going—a glass with a spoon in it ringing in the sink. The TV on in the next room. His only fall—from the easy chair to the rug, flopping about like a goldfish, gasping for air. His mouth, still open when she found him, wordless and twisted. The football fans cheering from the TV. A common death, like any other man.

CROSS-VENTILATION

We were watching a cowboy movie on the old black and white, where this guy, riding through a mountain pass, got ambushed from all sides. The bullets twisting him this way and that before he toppled from his horse. And my father said, *Cross ventilation*, and laughed. But I didn't understand, so he tried to explain his little joke. Something about open windows and metaphors and complementary air flows and punctures and how the cowboy that was shot… *Oh, forget it*, he said. And when my mother came in with two red potholder hands and asked him when he was going to fix something he'd been putting off for months, he flung back on the couch as if he'd been shot. Here, there and everywhere, spilling his beer on her plastic slipcovers and putting a hand over his heart, and said, *Cross ventilation*, as my mother looked at him and shook her head, and we both laughed. His deep one, and my giggly one. With only one of us knowing why.

THE WARM AND COZY

*C*an you imagine a peacock fight? he said, *two males squared off in a ring*. He pictured their feathers fanned out in spectacular display. Quivering. Catching the light that came in through barn slats at sharp angles. Guys around them shouting with fists squeezed around hard cash.

She was putting on her make-up, running late. Was a stripper at the *Warm & Cozy*, and listened with only half an ear. There'd be laps springing up, a long pole to slide down. Big smiles for big bucks. She heard something about cocks. A ring. *A cock ring?* she said. He looked up from the nature show he was watching. *No problem*, she said. *Whatever.*

He clicked off the set and got up to drive her, reminded her to speak to Roy about that bouncer position. *Sure*, she told him, knowing she never would. If he ever found out, she'd be the first one he bounced. *What's this about cock rings?* he said, holding the door open. A huge arm she ducked under. Hoping it wasn't a trick question.

UPRIGHT

His teen begged him to let her go to that concert and spend the night at a friend's. Standing there in her halter top and tight jeans—a billboard for all that defied him—as he cut his steak and looked up with boiling eyes. A father's *No way!* crimping his brow. Her *Why nots?* falling on deaf ears. Her mother, staring at the tines of her fork, and then a different look, as the father swallowed, knocking over his beer bottle. His eyes bugged out; red-faced and frantic, standing and scraping back his chair. The mother screaming. But only that. The father grabbing his throat. His teenager rushing him, reaching behind, as he nearly pushed her away. Her arms around him, barely, cupping her hands into a single fist and surging up into that loose belly. Adrenalin-grunts as she did. That half-chewed steak piece shooting out on the second, or was it the third try, into the serving plate. Into a bit of steak blood he planned on soaking up later with bread. Breathing finally and edging forward, away from her toward the table. Righting his bottle, as though the gesture meant something. That he was who he was. Righted. Lips parted, sucking air out of the room into him, saying between breaths: *Okay, okay, thanks. But don't you get any bright ideas that this changes anything, missy.*

A PURGATORY DWELLER'S GUIDE TO BIRD WATCHING

You come home from work with a tale to tell. For the kids. The wife. What happens on the elevator... How you... The claustrophobia/the release... The phone rings. The oven timer rings. The TV drowns you out. And the only thing that saves the day, besides the six-pack patient in the fridge, is when you walk the dog and turn, at just that right moment. See a sparrow high above the tree line, dive, as Edgar lifts a leg. Fifty caliber-bullet fast, landing inside a diamond in a chain link fence a foot away. Framed there for a moment, with a single eye on you, in a twitchy angled head. Then just as quickly, it jets off. Taking you with it.

BLOOD WATCH

The church elders were fussing over the IVs tubing into her father, checking each label against a list, to make sure none of the ingredients added up to *blood*. An ungodly transfusion that might, in sin, save him.

Two lines from Leviticus told them so: "*…no soul of you shall eat blood. Whoever eateth it shall be cut off.*"

The girl sat in the waiting area, as the women, her mother among them, curled into each other, discussing *God-matters*—nodding like bobble dolls. The girl clutched the *Magic 8-ball* given her by a cousin who wasn't in the faith. Peeked into her hands, as if she were cupping a bird.

Is there a heaven? she asked in her head, turning it. The die inside the globe floated up through blue liquid and pressed against the viewing window. *Very doubtful*, it read.

One of the women looked over. The girl put her hat over her hands. Will my father ever come back home? she asked. *Concentrate and ask again*. The girl closed her eyes. But all she could think of were the women leaned into each other like limp flowers. Will my father ever come home? *Better not tell you now*. The girl turned it a final time. Can I believe anything you say? *Outlook not so good*.

THE SPECIALIST

She was singing a song in Vietnamese which I found to be stunningly heartbreaking, even though I didn't understand a word of it. She sang softly as she looked at a small photo of my girlfriend, oceans away. A moment earlier, when we were done, she'd taken off her leg and leaned it against a cane chair in the corner. She'd become a specialist in oral pleasures because of it. *She number one pretty*, the girl said, rubbing a fingernail along a shock of red hair in the photo. I gave her a half-smile, wishing she would continue singing, but she didn't go back to it. My rifle leaned against the other side of the chair, only a little bit taller than the limb she'd left there. I slipped the picture in my wallet. Considered paying her to sing again. But knew it wouldn't be the same. The Sarge was in the next room over, and you could hear him banging away through the wall. It was a thin wall, and there was a radio playing.

BIG

He drove a monster truck in a big stadium on the weekends. The roar of cylinders and crowds still in his head days later. So high up. With such power under him, it was almost subterranean to sit in that overstuffed chair his father died in with a mystery book on his lap. Mickey Spillane, he recalled, with a single match for a bookmark. Something about a shotgun hole in someone so big, a baby could crawl through without ever getting its shoulders wet. And nothing good on TV, and their old cat just shit in his slipper. And his wife was pecking at him from the kitchen about God-knew-what. And, *Christ!*—the weekend just couldn't come quickly enough.

LURES, CEMENT AND OTHER DELICATE SUBJECTS

He lectured me on the limitless possibilities of *cement*. Was a new "uncle" my mother was seeing. There'd been many. I had to call them that. We were in a boat on the lake and he was showing me his lures collection. Held up each with a smile shiny as the hooks that hung from them. I was eleven and hated fish (except in bubbling tanks with blue sand and mermaids) and thought all cements created equal. A place to bounce a ball against, or spit at. But had to hear of its infinite virtues. How elegant the slog was pouring out of a twirling truck.

Later he would teach me how to fight. The way a tornado teaches a hen how to fly. My face reddened by the slaps I couldn't block in time. As tears formed, he said: *Are those girlie tears?* Got in another quick one. When I kicked him in the balls, and he folded like a lawn chair, his face blood-pooled; teeth-clenched, he said in a small, pinched voice: *Good. You got it, kid.* And we never returned to it again.

MILLIE IN ASCENDANCE

Millie was doing her nails in the parlor, when a part from a passing plane, crashed through the ceiling. Detaching like ordnance from a bomber. Altitude-frosted. Just missing her TV. Her favorite soap opera. The actors never missing a line, as Millie screamed and bolted from the house.

Millie, who worked the line at a frozen pizza plant, and was not acquainted with irony. Who never expected much out of life. Fame or fortune. Presented with the former, when the local media picked up the story and it went viral. Interviews on YouTube; telling how her Pomeranian, Mr. Bill, kept barking at it once he came out from behind the sofa.

And how it was just another day and she had a new bottle of *Atomic Orange* nail polish she was trying out. And Tiffany was breaking up with Mark on TV, and she never did get to see the look on his face when the *cheatin' son of a bitch got his*. But the airline was paying for the roof and rug, and then some. And ain't it funny how some things work out, not at all like you'd expect. And ain't it just crazy-mixed-up-really-something how it all can turn around on a dime.

SO THEY SAID

The chickens pecked around their steps as they headed back to the house. The sky lay low, brooding; charcoaled by rain. It would soon be more intimate. They'd just returned from an exorcism. A boy with one leg shorter than the other. Who didn't listen to his parents. Typed Satan-speak into his computer. Spoke sometimes in tongues. They said. All of them gathered around with *God-words*, and he told them to go fuck themselves. In a language they understood. They waited for the holy water to smoke and sizzle when it touched his skin. When it didn't, they headed home.

RED MEAT

I was seeing a widow who lived above the butcher shop back then. Taken with the way she curled her hair over one ear, how it slowly dropped back down again. She told me that her father had been a carnival barker. Of his fiery pitches. How they never stayed in one place for very long. That he was a quiet man, bookended by bottles of booze; a thick volume she couldn't crack open.

Only once mentioning her husband. Told me of the wild phase she went through as a teen. The plaster cast she made of a famous rock star's *Thing*. In a drawer now, under her delicates.

Afterward she'd sing to me in a foreign language. Hungarian, I think it was. Tunes that were haunting and soothing at the same time. I'd bring home pounds and pounds of meat later from the butcher downstairs. Thick red steaks and fat-veiny pork chops. Which my wife just stuffed in the freezer most times, without saying much.

JACKED UP

The two men couldn't find scorpions (like in those Spaghetti Westerns), tied to either end of a table — their stingers ominously curled, so they used a couple of jacks rooted from the toy box in her son's room, placing them where a losing hand might fall, and began arm wrestling. Needle-poked arms, one against the other.

Sitting by the window, she shook her head.

A biker rumbled by on his Harley and she imagined herself on back, arms around a thick waist going *anywhere*. Watching his collar flap like small wings. Plenty big enough.

She exhaled and smoke flattened against the glass. When she went over and scooped the jacks from the table, they both said: *Hey!* — still holding hands. She looked at them, her cigarette squinting one eye shut.

And somewhere was her man saying, *What the fuck?*

And somewhere was the TV going in her son's room.

And somewhere was the distance filing down the Harley into a little piece.

ANCIENT ALIENS

Traffic was stop-and-go for miles, and they were bickering again about his theories on extraterrestrial influences through time. How some of the most famous gunslingers of the Old West were really alien puppets, testing our capabilities. And how they've been at it from day one, when we were knuckle-scraping the ground, and how else could you explain half the weird and remarkable shit in this world. From antiquity, in particular.

And she knew better than to get into religion. So, at some point she just looked out at the creepy-crawly lanes of traffic, till they finally passed the long truck on its side, carrying a load of porta-potties. The cop cars, the flares, an ambulance. And it all sounded even sillier than usual. How there was so much to think about that didn't involve a visit from another planet. Was right there. Like the lump, for instance, she hadn't mentioned. Which was probably nothing. Just another bullet passing near without results. And, *Oh, Christ.* Not the pyramids. Not the goddamn pyramids again.

EVAPORATING LANDSCAPES

I stand before you like a man straightening his toupee after an unexpected wind. Dignity after all. You, like a boxer on spaghetti legs. A night dropping down; a hat so large it covers our eyes completely. It is 9:32 in the morning.

We are waiting for *The Call*. A doctor who likes playing with his eyeglasses when he speaks behind a big desk. An ocean liner desk, with us on the other side, sinking.

The phone rings. We let it. Then put it on speaker. Hear the good news. The torpedoes whizzing by. The phone click. The long hug. A quick change into something more comfortable. Sloppy and familiar. Something you swim in. Breaking the surface like a head through an old sweater. Sky and air and land, an inch away. The same terrain. The same terrain again. And, *Hey, what's for dinner?*

COLD LIGHT

Frank was a sewer worker. Was old enough to remember Ed Norton from *The Honeymooners*, being one. All the ribbing he took because of it. So he said he worked for the Water Department. Was beginning to date again. Went to a restaurant where the table candle was battery operated, nearly real-looking.

She told him she was a hand model when she was younger, and he noticed how balletic she made them, even with the simplest acts. That now she ran a vacuum cleaner repair shop, and if he said he bet it sucked, she'd crown him. They laughed and he saw she had something leafy between her teeth, but didn't know her well enough to mention it.

When there was a snag in the conversation, and those hands danced around the table touching things, lingering, he decided he didn't like the fake candle at all. Not because it wasn't interesting, but that he missed getting close sometimes and feeling the warmth, even the burn of the real thing. The way it moved with the slightest wind; the swing of an arm toward the salt. And that quick-vanishing flick of smoke when you blew it out. He liked that too.

Uneven Through the Petals

Jim tossed a piece of chicken into the pond out back. The school of piranhas attacked it with a bubbly agitation. A plum tree dropped a sprinkling of pink petals a few feet away. Jim's cat, Buster, walked unevenly through them with a bit of its front paw missing. The two men sat in beach chairs eating Kentucky Fried and drinking.

I never thought much about gravity, Jim said, *till Amy ripped the floor right out from under me.* He crushed his empty beer can and added it to some others in the grass. *Till she dumped me for that plumber dude. Hell, what plumber worth his salt does pipe sculptures?*

Amy always was a sucker for artsy stuff, Red said. The cat walked gingerly past the pond.

Maybe I should have taken up macramé.

Finger painting's more like it, Red said, and they both laughed. Flung a few more pieces and watched the aquatic mayhem.

The cat gazed at a small speck of chicken skin at the lip of the pond, as if considering it, then plopped over and licked a few petals from its back instead.

PRISONERS OF MOMENTUM

I'll bet shape shifters are fun in bed, she says, as we watch some apes in their habitat. One, a large male, engaged in a half-hearted charge.

That's strange, Beth, I say. *You tryin' to tell me something?*

It just occurred to me, it might be exciting. You'd never know who was going to show up.

I was the tail end of a pantomime horse once, I tell her. *That count?*

She snaps off a piece of pink popcorn and puts it between her lips, smiles. I wonder if things are getting old for her. Stale as that popcorn. If I need to beat my chest more. Maybe roar a little. I think how comfortable routines can be. How insidious. Consider asking her what new shape she might prefer. Various possibilities flit in my brain like those birds in the aviary across from us. Think better of it, and we move on. Watch a hippo lumber up to a small pool and transform, momentarily; balletic in the water. Close as it gets sometimes.

GIANTS THAT COULDN'T SPEAK

I was sixteen and we were on our way to the drive-in—giants flicking in the dark from the highway. Silently moving their lips. Something magical. Something sad. Where the mall is now.

She sat beside me chewing gum (three slices, one after another) with her mouth open. It was a pretty mouth. She didn't need to advertise. Told me she could tie a knot in a cherry stem using her tongue. Said it with a bright-eyed intimation. I told her that would be really something. She asked if I wanted to bet. Bet she couldn't do it. *Ten million*, I said. She told me I could do better. I thought about that. We went through a tunnel, and the chewing got louder. Even her perfume was loud. A floral scream. I cracked open a window.

Ms. Fix-It

He was in there smoking weed again, with towels pushed against the bottom of the door. But she could smell it anyway. That sharp scent cutting through the remnants of her morning coffee. Then the deep, guttural sounds of his Tuvan throat singing. Otherworldly, and resonant. His fourteen-year-old peep-tone voice plummeting. Like the CDs he played, which sounded to her too much like devils chanting with frogs in their throats. *You hungry?* she asked through the door. Her hands hungry to make something. His *No!* soaring back several octaves.

She returned to the kitchen and put on another pot. There was sunlight on her azaleas out back, needing to be watered. There was the cat brushing her leg for food. There were still a few teen years left. She sprinkled fishy stars into a bowl till they spilled over. Some things were just easier to fix than others.

WHEN WINGS ARE NOT ENOUGH

The skeleton sat on the couch drinking whiskey straight from the bottle. On the coffee table was a cage filled with parakeets. He thought he could tell what they were saying. Especially the blue one, the loudest. Its melodious rant. Figured *escape* was involved.

The skeleton suit from five Halloweens ago fit tightly. He kept pulling at his crotch. When Cindy came home with the girls, he'd stand and model the boney outfit. Remind her how she was always saying he should lose weight. That was Roger, always good for a laugh. He missed his job at the plant. The guys, the back and forth. He and Spanky (their old tomcat) were beasts amongst the blooms. Hoped the tuneful chirping might smooth things.

He thought to set the blue one free. Then reconsidered. Sometimes wings were not enough. The cat stared into the cage. He shooed it away with his Halloween hand. It edged back a little. Sparks and tinder in its eyes. Even as it licked itself, to demonstrate nonchalance. Even as Roger took a swig and shook a fist.

TRICKLING OUT

Jake's wife, Carol, had taken the small hourglass from their kid's Boggle game and was stating her issues. In that meager time-frame, just like the young couples therapist with Pocahontas braids had instructed. Their *homework*.

He was missing the fight on TV, two up-and-comer middle-weights going at it, while he intermittently watched her lips, then the sand, or whatever it was, trickling down to the bottom of the timer. Wondered how they could get something so fine through a hole so small. If only life spilled out as predictably. Occasionally he'd nod as she went on. Something about a fairer distribution of work around the house, and how he watched too much TV. He glanced at the piling seconds.

Thought about the nicknames some of these boxers had: *The Motor City Cobra*, *The Baby-faced Assassin*—John, *The Beast*, Mugabi. Thought, perhaps, his might be something like Jake, *The Trickle-Watcher*. Or *Stuck On This Damn Couch Bored Out of My Gourd*, Jake could be on the marquee. When the last particle had topped the snowy pyramid, his wife said, *Great. You did well.* Then Carol, *The Pitiless Nut-Crusher*, turned the little timer over, and it was his turn to talk.

BRANDED

She picks the lock on her daughter's diary. Nearly chokes on her own saliva at a passage describing an older boy leaving the imprint of his gold crucifix on her left breast—his weight upon her. And the size of it (not the crucifix). And the mother's Chicken Fricassee, she always said she loved. How she fed it to the dog. And that road trip to Niagara Falls, how she couldn't stop thinking of him/them the whole time, and who cared about a bunch of stupid water falling down. How it was just a lot of *oohs* and *ahhs* over not much at all. And she knew now what really mattered. And she wasn't their little girl anymore. But still kept her stuffed animals on the bed anyway. For appearance's sake. Except for a few she still liked being there. And, hey, that was okay too.

FINGERING THE WORDS

Elegantly dressed, she sat reading from a book of poems in Braille. Her sunglasses on the coffee table. It was our second date, and the first time I'd seen her with them off. She read me a surreal one about Einstein's brain talking into Van Gogh's ear at a local steak house, and we laughed.

Her cat crouched on the backrest of the sofa and stared out at the bird bath; at poetry it wanted to still. She crossed her legs and asked if I wanted to hear another. I nodded, then caught myself. *You bet*, I said.

The next one was a fable about a king who built an hourglass big enough to last a thousand years. I got up and sat between her and the cat, and she smiled without stopping when the couch cushion compressed. It was twilight and would soon be dark. I wondered if she would think to turn on the lamp, or if I'd have to stumble over and do it.

CANNED LAUGHTER

(In Translation)

It helped when she thought of her situation as a sitcom. An old one—'60s, '70s. The brute revving his motorcycle out front for her daughter, as *The Fonz*; hard-shelled, but soft on the inside. The devil and dagger tattoos, as something they put on with a wet sponge over in Props. The canned laughter in the background as she sat at the kitchen table alone. Tapped her cigarette ash into an empty pie tin and yelled in her teenage daughter's wake—at the red skirt too high up. *Make sure you wear a helmet!*

The: *Yeah, yeah,* like small seeds you spit out from a sour orange. And from the canned laughter, always that one guffaw louder than the rest. Her mother's, say, from the afterlife. Nearly a cackle one might hear (in translation)—sharp as the lid from a just opened can. Old, yet fresh: *Okay, smarty pants, you'll see someday, when you have kids of your own. Just you wait...*

WEIGHTS AND MEASURES

My great aunt, Rose, raised turtles in her backyard. Slow-motion ramblings, which said much about the tempo of her own life. When we'd visit, her long accounts, equally plodding. As we sipped chamomile she poured from a crazed pot. Translating memory and matter into something quantitive, sure. As we listened; the drowsy creep of life forms through the grass. Dates, times of day; the depth of the whiskey in a glass left on the table. A man once. A monster, say. *Godzilla*. How tall. The number of scales on its back. How exquisite in sunlight. How fracturingly deadly. How handsome. How much, in tonnage, it/he might have weighed.

HAND SHADOWS

My old knuckles ache, piled one atop the other: the tightly structured goose I try to animate; too long past any chance of wizardry. A smeared and feckless shadow on the wall. The same with each that follows—wing-beats and flapping jaws and squeaky cartoon talk without a laugh or twinkle from my daughter. A cycle of magic and its opposite playing out. Impossible to know when the change occurred. When the turkey or the silly duck became a hand—the *shadow* of a hand and nothing more.

ZOOLAND

All day he shoveled dung at the zoo. A life viewed through cages and bars. Wore too much Aqua Velva for his young wife's asthma. She still remembered him, Mountain-high, on that lifeguard tower. The salty/cocoa butter scent of him in the sheets. *The elephants,* he'd told her. *Christ!—the elephants...* She was humming a tune from a TV commercial which had stuck in her head. He asked her to stop. There was a roast in the oven, a canary making a racket in the sunroom, their toddler forming an army of wide-jawed alligator clothespins. He got up and reached for the remote sprouting from between the couch cushions where she sat. Leaned close and plucked it out like a radish. Sat back in his Lazy Boy. She coughed.

THE BIRDS NEVER CAME

When he retired, he made birdhouses. Ornate ones. The Taj Mahal of birdhouses. A couple in every tree. And when he ran out of trees, he banged in posts and hung them. There was little space left in the yard that didn't hold an aviary splendor. But the birds never came. *Maybe a birdbath*, she said. *Maybe that would bring them.*

But it was his hands, he told her. It wasn't about the birds. It was the saw, the hammer; those little nails. The glue he peeled from his fingers like sun-burnt skin, and the carvings; the planing; the spin of the vise clenching its teeth. It was the small cans of paint he opened and closed. It was the sandpaper and the miniature shingles. The brushes he washed, and the wood dust he swept up in little pyramids. It was his hands that needed filling. Not the houses. It was never about the birds.

INTERPRETER OF DREAMS

My mother was the self-appointed interpreter of dreams; coughing out her verdicts with an early morning smoke. Mining her slumber for forecasts: silverware meant guests were coming—hands: a gift; bees represented bad luck (especially if they were swarming) and "teeth"—the one we dreaded most, meant *certain death*. And it didn't matter whose: a family member, a neighbor, even old movie stars counted, were not safe, and we'd wait for the ax to fall, and of course, it always did and she'd say: *See!* The Rosetta Stone she carried in her head, infallible back then. As we listened with our spoons frozen over cold bowls of cereal. She, in her robe, with her coffee and her cigarettes and the fate of the world in her hands.

VITAMIN EXPRESS

*T*here are no guardrails in Hell, you say, studying a bottle at Vitamin Express. Tap a lacquered fingernail against it. I straighten from a bottom shelf.

Ever notice how metaphors start to look like the people that use them after a while? The way certain pets look like their owners? I say.

Humm, you muse, shaking the bottle almost musically. *Hope is like a pair of old socks on the line,* you tell me. *Horizontal and plump with wind.* I can't tell whether she looks more like the socks or the wind. I have my doubts these bottles will ever give us what we are seeking.

The woman behind the counter points at the Economy-Size section, and tells us they're kinder on the pocketbook. She has a look, like ocean-tamed beach glass. Smooth, inviting.

Even a dozen fat angels cannot buckle the sky, I tell my girlfriend, straining to lift a bottle onto the counter, as she measures the words against my countenance.

Pretty in sunlight, and saltwater-fresh, the cashier rings us up.

IN THE SWING OF THINGS

He got on Antiques Road Show with an old broach his grandmother left him. Keeps playing that tape of him gawking into the camera and saying, *Oh, wow* a lot. I've watched it four times already, and it is on again as he gets us each a cold one.

Little more than a year ago, I pulled his head from a bowl of chowder. He'd been taking barbiturates after a breakup, and I grabbed him by the hair in a restaurant and had to slap him awake outside in the cold. Walk him with a stranger; his limp arms on our shoulders. And now he was a celebrity, and Nina was coming over later to cheer him up further. This back and forth of the metronome. Too fast, too slow. Sometimes, just right.

Oh, wow, he says. *Oh, wow!* On the 60 inch screen, close up, as a neatly-suited gentleman points to a cluster of diamonds and comments on their clarity.

SO MUCH CHANGES,
SO MUCH STAYS THE SAME

In the car she's telling me what it would be like if Iran got nuclear weapons. A Joni Mitchell song is playing, and Joni is blue as if she were listening. *Can you imagine?* she says. *Fuck.* I'm thinking about my in-laws at the other end of this highway. The turkey, the table exploding.

•••

Will you look at that, my mother said once, holding open a '50s magazine. Pointing to the fancy fallout shelter; the smiling family in their perfect world. *Better Homes and Gardens* perfect. And I tried to squeeze what she was saying into the little space I had for such things. Pushing out stickball and marbles, to make room for blood-boiling light. *Like the Ritz,* my mother said.

•••

Well, let's hope, I say.

Hope what?

Hope they don't get them.

Hope, hell, she tells me, as though I'd gotten all the answers wrong to a quiz. I'm waiting for Joni to cheer up. *Christ,* nobody plays a sledge hammer better. There is macro. There is micro. Whatever fits. Outside it is sunny. There are wildflowers, then an accident in the traffic going the other way. Wildflowers again.

THE LONG MILES TO ARIZONA

He'd packed his racing pigeons, what were left of them, in the screened travel box the long miles to Arizona. Kept a gun under the seat. Commented on the small dust devils that scooped up out of nowhere, and died as quickly. She kept telling him she saw a roadrunner, but when he turned it wasn't there. A moving van had taken the bulk of their belongings a week earlier, and now they dragged along a small trailer behind them like a piece of toilet paper stuck to a shoe. Filled with meaningless incidentals and his birds; the two that survived.

He reminded her how close to the casinos they'd be. And how they could kiss those Chicago blizzards goodbye. But she just stared straight ahead. After a bit, she said she saw a fish shaped into the purple mountains against the horizon. With its mouth open. He pictured it gulping. He told her he saw Lincoln's head in profile. *Like on a penny*, he said. *A lucky one.*

16 Wheeler

Entering the kitchen, he found the rooster in his cereal bowl scratching about. She was in her robe watching the small TV on the counter. An Italian cooking show, where a stout woman in a flowered dress, kept kissing her pinched fingers up to heaven after every dish.

"Git!" he said, shooing it off the table and out through a tear in the screen door.

Now it was her silence smacking into him like a 16 wheeler. Wondered how in the hell she managed to squeeze his philandering out of him. Probably the booze talking.

He glanced up through the mesh. At a low, brooding sky. "Looks like rain," he said. "Least we'll get that old heap washed."

She switched the channel. On a kid's show, a plush dinosaur was speaking in a goofy manner, waving clawless stunted arms. She laughed.

PRETTY BOY

She lived by the ocean and when she wasn't blasting her music, you could hear the waves crashing in. She had thick lips, perfectly painted, was always checking them out, puckering, touching them up. Had a talking bird named Pretty Boy, that would watch us tangled in the sheets. Said, *Asshole!* a lot—stretching out its wings. Which I never liked, but always made her laugh. It sat beside her; shells from seeds in wreckage on the couch. Its sudden green gusts above my head, then back again. In its cage one night, with the cover over it as she slept, I heard it say: *Pretty Boy.* Softly. Just once, just that. In the darkness: its/my own.

THE OTHER SIX RINGS

My eight-year-old gyrates two hula hoops into orbits and keeps them there. Says she is Saturn. That she's learned about planets in school. Breathless, she tells me Saturn has 8 rings, but she is a little Saturn, so only has two. I tell her two are plenty. And how pleased I am that this fine planet has visited our living room with such a grand display.

•••

She works in the glove department at Nordstrom's now. Says how sick she is of hands, of leather. My little planet with a planet of her own. A son who draws eyes everywhere. Even his Mr. Potato Head has only the eyes pushed into it. Wonders if she should be concerned. Or wave it off like that last white puff from a bag of flour.

•••

And I wonder if you ever stop being a parent. Waiting for the other six rings to spin in place. Or a nose, a smiling mouth to appear. Ears to hear the footsteps coming. Whomever they belong to. Whatever it is they carry.

UNBROKEN

She was sitting on a blanket in the sand playing a violin. A seagull serenade perhaps. For the gulls were landing nearby, abandoning a sea full of fish. The Cheetos bag on my own blanket spilled open beside the broken sand dollars my daughter collected. And I thought of my father, those late years, filling the yard with broken things. Porcelain rabbits with ears missing by my stepmother's asters. A headless angel by her blazing stars.

She was in a bikini and the fervent tones, the coconut-butter-wind, the waves, were in seamless integration. I was playing *Name That Tune* and failing, but it didn't matter. I wondered if there was a broken heart involved or something mended but remembered. I shut my eyes. My wife and daughter would soon be back with wet stones, shell pieces and broken glass, the sea's alchemy would transform. Funny, I thought, what context frames. What makes things whole again.

ABOUT THE AUTHOR

Robert Scotellaro has been published widely in national and international books, journals and anthologies. He is the author of seven literary chapbooks and several books for children. His story "Fun House" is included in the anthology *Flash Fiction International* by W.W. Norton. A collection of his flash fiction, *Measuring the Distance*, was published by Blue Light Press (2012). He was the recipient of Zone 3's Rainmaker Award in Poetry. With Dale Wisely, he co-edits the journal, *One Sentence Poems*. Raised in Manhattan, he currently lives with his wife in San Francisco. Visit him at www.rsflashfiction.com. He can be reached at rtscotellaro@gmail.com.

www.ingramcontent.com/pod-product-compliance
Lightning Source LLC
Chambersburg PA
CBHW032028090426
42741CB00006B/775